Herstellung und Verlag:

© 2019
Herstellung und Verlag: BoD – Books on Demand, Norderstedt.
ISBN:
9783749450763

Copyright:
© 2019 Taylor E. Baxter, Erstveröffentlichung 22.04.2019

# Foreword

Do you want more creativity and ingenuity from your game management?

Do you play the same game modes on a regular basis, even though your finger itches to try something else?

Here you will find a number of game modes with essential information.

## Do you organize games by yourself?

Read through the game modes presented and think about which you think are feasible. Don't be afraid to adapt and transform them into your players.

Surprise your players with new, innovative ideas!

Almost all players appreciate proving their skills in different game variations. That's why the game modes presented here range from Speedgame classics (Team Deathmatch) to different scenarios!

Player wants fun - make sure they get it! Challenge them with new challenges!

Give your games your personal "fingerprint" - be creative!

# the game modes

Airsoft offers a wide variety of game modes - not least due to the inventiveness and creativity of the game management and organizers.

Creative minds get plenty of inspiration from video games and movies. They let players be the heroes in their own story.

Speed game fans appreciate high "hit rates". MilSim fans, on the other hand, enjoy more tactical elements and components that give them the feeling of staying in the middle of the action of a "campaign".

*Game leaders offer players the opportunity to feel like heroes.*

Similar to the stories of wizards and dragons in medieval hero epics, in Airsoft it is elite units, snipers and other "characters" who win campaigns and emerge victorious from their missions.

*General Tips*

Organize the required equipment. The demand varies according to the game mode. If you think about experimenting more, it makes sense to put together a piece of "basic equipment"!

## Usable basic equipment:

- Different coloured loops
- Flags
- Notepads and writing materials
- Timer / Chess clocks
- Material for barricades
- Material for staking out (ribbons, flags, ...)
- Containers of different sizes
- Marble and/or pebbles
- Briefcase

If you adapt game modes, add the intended equipment to your list. In the course of time you will get an exceptionally well-filled fund.

## Game modes

For the sake of simplicity, the groups in this book are called "Team". You are free to name them "squad", "unit" or otherwise.

Make sure you have a sufficient number of arm loops in different colors.

## Tip:

Usually, game leaders use bright or clearly visible colors. Try earthier and/or darker colors. The affiliation remains, but the MilSims players do not stand out too clearly from camouflage and/or hiding.

Especially with FFAs, you'll find similar modes like "Team Deathmatch", because they've been tried and tested. This is a useful idea in view of the regular arrival of new players, which you can adapt at any time. Take familiar game modes and change them. Build on the presented modes and add new, unexpected things. Don't slavishly adhere to the rules, do your own thing!

- *complexity:*

  Level of difficulty - varies according to playing experience

- *game environment:*

  Which environment is particularly suitable?

- *Required:*

  What do you need for this mode?

- *Scenario:*

  The starting point

- *Game content:*

  What is it about and how is the mode to be executed?

- *Game objective:*

  What should the players achieve?

- *Comment for the administrator:*

  General information, tips, tricks and more!

You can adjust, complicate or facilitate every single aspect. Look at the guidelines as a "starting point" for your own ideas!

# 1. Last man standing

## Complexity:

1 of 10

## Game environment:

open spaces, woods, meadows, halls, houses

## Required:

- ✓ from 2 players up

## Game content:

- ➤ The players start from different places on the playground.
- ➤ Every player hit leaves the playing field - everyone has a life.
- ➤ There are no allies and no friends, everyone "fights" for himself!

## Game objective:

This mode is won by the last player on the playing field!

## Note for the administrator:

This game mode is one of the most popular. Especially on FFA (Free for all) events "Last man standing" is part of the standard repertoire! Easy to comprehend and without any material, it makes pure fun possible!

# 2. One in the Chamber

## Complexity:

3 of 10

## Game environment:

open spaces, woods, meadows, halls, houses

## Required:

✓ from 2 players up

## Game content:

➢ The players start from different places on the playground.

➢ One BB per player is allowed.

    –> Therefore a targeted meeting is important!

➢ If the player meets the BB, he may load a new BB into the magazine.

➢ If you shoot your BB without hitting it, you have to be in the "Close combat! By "knife" or "shoot" there is the possibility to catapult opponents out of the game.

➢ If he manages to "knife" an opponent or to

➢ "Shoot", the player may fill another BB into the magazine.

## Game objective:

This mode is won by the last player on the playing field.

## Note for the administrator:

This game mode works best with fair players or when the players know each other. Without confidence in the honesty, this game mode will not work.

Tell players that it is essential that there is never more than one BB in the magazine.

Do not recommend players to use markers that only work in Full Auto mode. Machine guns and similar models cannot be filled quickly enough in the heat of battle!

_Variant:_

Hide on the field several small containers filled with 10 BB each. Whoever finds them has the right to immediately fill them into his magazine and shoot them in one piece.

Make sure WHO finds the containers by removing the container from the player in question. Number the containers! If at the end of this game mode the containers remain on the ground, a scavenger hunt is the best option!

Whoever finds the most containers wins!

# 3. Lonely Wolf

## Complexity:

2 of 10

## Game environment:

open spaces, forest, houses, halls

## Required:

- ✓ from 3 players up
- ✓ 1 single player against all

## Game content:

- ➢ 1 single player volunteers!
- ➢ This player will compete against all other players.

  *»Lonely Wolf«* -> 3 lifes

  *Antagonist* -> 1 Life

## Game objective:

The "Lonely Wolf" wins as soon as he removes all antagonists from the game!

## Note for the administrator:

This game mode is suitable for all players who like to be the center of attention. With luck, the "Lone Wolf."

### Referral:

- o Keep a minimum of "balance" to avoid frustration.

- o Restriction to a certain number of players

- o Restriction of "marker selection"

*Variant:*

Link the Solitary Wolf game mode to a creative task. Give them different choices and possibilities. Let his puzzle.

A busy "Lone Wolf" can accomplish his task if he is good enough or disguises himself well enough. If you have too many enemies for the "Solitary Wolf", put a "helper" aside - for example, a mole of which he doesn't know anything in the beginning.

- o *Hostage Liberation*:
  The Lone Wolf frees a hostage and takes them to safety.

- o *Prison break*
  Overpower his guards and escape into safe respawn - with a rubber or latex knife and a sidearm

- o *Sharpshooter*:
  Mission accomplished - target eliminated - he must get to safety before the other side brings him to justice.

# 4. find the Terrorist

## Complexity:

4 of 10

## Game environment:

Meadow, forest, houses

## Required:

✓ from 3 players up

## Game content:

➤ 1 single player volunteers! He may carry with him whatever equipment and ammunition he likes.

➤ Before the game starts, the "terrorist" hides on the playing field.

➤ All other players are part of the Counter Terrorist Team. Their task is to find and eliminate the "terrorist".

➤ Each member of the Counter-Terrorist-Team has 3 lives. After a hit is a search for the "Respawn" necessary, there is no waiting time in the "Respawn.

## Game objective:

1 player against all - the terrorist is hit or his antagonist are all out of play.

## Note for the administrator:

Sharpen the game mode by allowing the "Counter-Terrorist Team" only one sidearm.

The "Terrorist" is allowed any material. He must wear it if he plans to change his hiding place.

# 5. Counterkill-Parcour

## Complexity:

1 of 10

## Game environment:

forest, meadow, houses, hall

## Required:

- ✓ from 8 - 10 players
- ✓ Material to "limit" a course (pennants, flags, ribbons, ...)
- ✓ Timer

## Game content:

- ➢ Stake out a suitable course.
- ➢ Choose a player! This player has to wait in the safe zone!
- ➢ Assign fixed positions outside the course to the other players. You may not move more than 2 m away from these fixed points.
- ➢ Send the player to the start. His task is to fight his way through the course. Activate the timer when it starts. If he leaves the course, he has lost.
- ➢ After the fifth hit, the solo player is outside. The remaining players have a life.

## Game objective:

Achieve the highest score!

## Note for the administrator:

This game mode is similar to the principle of various ego shooters. It works even better when you have more players at your disposal. Draw the order of the solo players! The previous solo player takes the place of the new solo player. The game mode ends as soon as everyone has crossed the course once. Mix up the fixed positions regularly.

### Attention:

The Complexity consists of the task for the game leader with the point calculation. The calculation list is a suggestion. Change it as you like.

### Calculation:

Per eliminated opponent: +5 points per safepoint reached: +10 points

### Extra points:

All Safepoints: +30 Points / all opponents fired out: +70 Points

### Penalty points:

Hit - per hit: -5 Points / completely out: -10 Points

### Time:

after own measurement

# 6. Vietnam

## Complexity:

3 of 10

## Game environment:

open spaces, woods, meadows, halls, houses

## Required:

- ✓ from 4 players upwards
- ✓ per player loops in two different colours - or with turning possibility

## Game content:

- ➢ Split the players into two teams.
- ➢ As soon as a player is hit, he changes teams! This changes the proportions of the teams!

## Game objective:

All players are in the same group!

## Note for the administrator:

Give each player two loops or trust the honesty of the players. Instruct them to change the color of the loops when they change teams!

# 7. gladiator fight

## Complexity:

4 of 10

## Game environment:

smaller playing area, limited space such as a hall or a small piece of forest

### Prerequisite

must be equally easy to enter and leave from both sides

## Required:

- ✓ 2 - 10 players
- ✓ Timer adjustable to 2 minutes
- ✓ 1 shrill pipe

## Game content:

- ➢ Split the players into two teams.
- ➢ Give them the starting points.
- ➢ Each team determines the order in which its members enter the field!
- ➢ As soon as the teams have taken their places, the game management gives the starting signal.
- ➢ The selected "Player A" of both teams start simultaneously. They have two minutes to cross the playing field and reach the

opposite end. Whoever succeeds first wins and moves on. The loser is eliminated.

*Attention:*

If one of the players is hit, he loses.

➤ Afterward, the following players (B, C, D, ...) get their chance - also limited to 2 minutes each!

➤ Once all the players have gone through, the second round with the winners will begin.

➤ You make another choice about the order.

➤ They will again get two minutes for each "pair".

➤ If the number of players is odd, one player may play 2x as "Joker".

## Game objective:

The winner is the team with "surviving" players.

## Note for the administrator:

Be careful not to exceed the number of 10 players. Players want to be active, too long waiting times are a nuisance. If none of the "pair" manages to cross the area within the given time, both players emerge from the round as "winners" or "losers". This decision is made by the game management.

*Referral:*

Proceed in the same way with all "draws".

# 8. Team Deathmatch – TMD

## Complexity:

1 of 10

## Game environment:

meadows, forest, gravel pits, houses, halls

## Required:

✓ from 4 players

## Game content:

➢ Split the players into two teams.

➢ Both teams start simultaneously from their respective respawn.

➢ If a player gets a hit, he has to leave the field immediately.

## Game objective:

The last team with a "survivor" wins.

## Note for the administrator:

The game mode is particularly suitable for newcomers, or when players prefer simpler game modes where the tactical component is less clearly represented.

# 9. Respawn Deathmatch

## Complexity:

3 of 10

## Game environment:

meadows, forest, gravel pits, houses, halls

## Required:

- ✓ from 6 players
- ✓ 2 containers (washed-out cans are ideally suited) sufficient BB or pebbles that the assistant dispenses

## Game content:

- ➤ Appoint two players as your assistants and send them to respawn separately. They place themselves 5 m away from the respawn. Give them containers.
- ➤ Divide the remaining players into two teams.
- ➤ The teams start simultaneously.
- ➤ For each hit a player collects, he goes to his own respawn and throws a BB or pebble into the can.
- ➤ The assistant hands them to him!
- ➤ If a player succeeds in reaching the opponent's respawn without being hit himself, the assistant will pass 10 BB or pebbles to this player.

> The player throws these BB or pebbles into the opposing team's pot. In "Off Mode", the player goes into his own respawn with his hand raised, without placing a BB or pebble there, and restarts the game.

## Game objective:

The team with the fewest BB or pebbles in the pot wins!

## Note for the administrator:

Every player has an infinite number of lives. Limit the game time to 30 minutes.

### Variant:

Hide flags on the field. Make sure they represent different countries. Which countries you choose doesn't matter! Assign a concrete number of BB or pebbles to each flag. The account will then be settled. This ensures that the players remain in the dark until the end - the bigger the surprise!

### eine mögliche Aufteilung:

10 BB – flag USA

5 BB – flag Germany

3 BB – flag UDSSR

1 BB – flag Japan

0 BB – flag Canada

-3 BB – flag Alaska

- 10 BB – flag Siberia

# 10. Sniper and Spotter

## Complexity:

3 of 10

## Game environment:

wood, meadow, gravel pit, houses, halls

## Required:

✓  from 4 players upwards

## Game content:

➤  Select two players and send them to the terrain, where they position themselves as "snipers and observers".

➤  After 5 minutes, send the remaining players to the terrain. Each of them has the task to eliminate the sniper and his observer.

## Game objective:

The last team with a „survivor" wins.

## Note for the administrator:

Prefer those players for the team of two who have at least one ghillie.

# 11. Collect it!

## Complexity:

3 of 10

## Game environment:

meadown, wood, gravel pit, houses, halls

## Required:

- ✓ from 10 players
- ✓ 4 tapes per player

## Game content:

- ➤ Appoint two players as your assistants and send them to respawn in advance.
- ➤ Give each player 4 ribbons. These should be worn on the left shoulder.
- ➤ Split the players into two teams.
- ➤ If a hit is made, the player must loosen one of the bands and hand it over to the shooter. If it is unclear who the shooter was, the tape must be placed on the spot where it was when the goal was scored.
- ➤ The shooter picks up the tape and puts it to his own.
- ➤ If a player loses his last tape, he must leave the playing area. If he finds a "forgotten" tape on the floor on his way back, he gets another life!

## Game objective:

The team loses without tapes!

## Note for the administrator:

It happens that players place the ribbons on the ground because they cannot identify the shooter.

The ribbons remain on the ground. Attentive players have the opportunity to gain an extra life.

For each respawn visit, players must hand over a tape to the assistant.

### Variant:

Distribute a handful of ribbons on the playing area before the game. Mark them with numbers or letters to distinguish them from the "normally" distributed ribbons.

Anyone who discovers and collects these specially marked ribbons will receive extra points at the final scoring or exchange these ribbons with the Respawn Wizard. Per special band the player receives 5 "normal" bands - per "normal" band, there is 1 extra life!

Distribute further objects on the terrain, which can be used against "normal" ribbons and are therefore exchangeable for extra life

# 12. Wolfpack

## Complexity:

2 of 10

## Game environment:

Open space, wood, meadown, halls, houses

## Required:

✓ from 4 player upwards

## Game content:

➢ The players start from different places on the playground.

➢ When the game starts, each player tries to hit any number of others.

➢ Every player hit joins his shooter immediately after he has noted "HIT". Each successful hit reinforces your own page.

➢ Who is in the common team, fires itself no more! A change into another team is still possible.

➢ Players of one team stay close to each other. Thus they are more clearly recognizable as a team.

## Game objective:

All players are in one group!

## Note for the administrator:

It's up to you if you want to give them bows of different colors.

I'll let you have it. In the case of smaller groups, "markings" are often unnecessary.

If you limit this game mode to 15 minutes, the team with the highest number of players wins the final whistle. Leave the resulting teams together for the next game mode! If the division is too different, choose a mode that has teams of different sizes Required!

### Variant:

Draw two players for the task of the lead wolf. Their task is to get the dominant wolf pack.

### Alternativ:

Divide the players into teams of two before the game starts! Let the players draw pieces of paper with numbers from a closed container.

Many teams and groups train together. With this method, you throw the usual groups in a mess. Those who have played together often do not know how to assess their "new" partner - at the same time, they know how their "accustomed" partner acts and proceeds.

# 13. Tree changes!

## Complexity:

2 of 10

## Game environment:

meadown, wood, gravel pit, houses, halls

## Required:

- ✓ from 4 players
- ✓ 1 container containing several labels bearing the number 1 or the number 2

## Game content:

- ➢ Split the players into two teams.
- ➢ Players hit hurry to the starting base and pull one of the numbers slips out of the container. Who draws a 1 - belongs to the team of 1 and vice versa.

## Game objective:

The team with the last players on the field wins.

## Note for the administrator:

Divide the numbers on the slips evenly. This gives each team sufficient chances to move in. If there are no more pieces of paper, the players receive no more lives and wait in the starting base for the end of the game.

# 14. Captainshunt

## Complexity:

4 of 10

## Game environment:

wood, meadow, houses, halls

## Required:

- ✓ from 10 players
- ✓ 2 clearly visible markings for the captains
- ✓ 1 megaphone or a correspondingly loud voice!

## Game content:

- ➤ Split the players into two teams.
- ➤ Each team appoints a leader - the Captain. The captain is to be announced to the opposing team.
- ➤ Give the markings to the captains. Helmet markings are suitable, since most players wear helmets in the meantime!
- ➤ Starting from the start whistle, the only task the players have to perform is the "to meet with the Captain.
- ➤ Every player has as many lives as he wants, except for the Captain. With him a single hit is enough and the game is over!
- ➤ The captain must show himself openly as soon as you give the command!

Game objective:

Whoever takes out the opposing captain first wins.

## *Note for the administrator:*

Many players tend to bunk in. To prevent this, the "Captain" has to move. Give him two to four points on the terrain between which he has to commute constantly. There he has to touch the respective point briefly and start again immediately.

He is free to camouflage himself and/or to use different movement patterns - as long as he has his

"Marking" visible!

You need assistants who can observe this by watching from a certain height (tower, building top, ...) or by standing and waiting at the fixed points.

### *Variant:*

> If the captain manages to survive 10 minutes without hitting the target, he may appoint another player to replace him as captain.

# 15. Capture the flag

## Complexity:

3 of 10

## Game environment:

open areas like meadown with coverings or gravel pit

## Required:

- ✓ from 2 players
- ✓ flags

## Game content:

- ➤ Put the flags into the ground 5 meters before the respawns of the teams.
- ➤ Split the players into two teams.
- ➤ Each team should conquer the opponent's flag - at the same time, their own flag should be protected from the opponent.
- ➤ The players are free to carry and/or throw the flag.

    ### Attention:

    If the flag bearer is hit, he shall leave the flag on the spot and go to respawn. It is forbidden to move and/or throw the flag after a hit!

## Game objective:

Conquering the enemy flag!

It counts who holds the flag in his hands at the end of the given time.

## Note for the administrator:

Instead of classic flags, you can use "reversible flags". You need a stick and 2 different colored cloths (for example green and purple). Fix them to the opposite ends of the stick.

Well-rehearsed teams score points because they know each other well enough to know what their own team member can do.

You create increased suspense with a concrete timeline that you must adhere to!

### Variant:

Let the teams hide their own flags. In this mode, players may take "prisoners" and ask for the flag's location.

For this variant, you give the flag to the teams instead of putting it into the ground.

Let the players decide for themselves who hides the flag! This player is only allowed to play with his sidearm - a fast runner makes sense!

# 16. battle for the flag

## Complexity:

2 of 10

## Game environment:

open areas like meadown with coverings or gravel pit

## Required:

- ✓ only "armed" with the Sidearm
- ✓ 1 flag

## Game content:

- ➤ Place the flag in the middle of the pitch.
- ➤ Split the players into two teams.
- ➤ Each team shall endeavor to conquer the flag and bring it into their own respawn.
- ➤ Players are free to carry and/or throw the flag.

  ### Attention:

  If the flag bearer is hit, he shall leave the flag on the spot and go to respawn. It is forbidden to move and/or throw the flag after a hit!

## Game objective:

It counts who holds the flag in his hands at the end of the given time.

## Note for the administrator:

Well-rehearsed teams score points because they know each other well enough to know what their own team member can do.

You'll create more excitement with a specific timeline to keep!

Allow players to use their "normal" markers.

### Variant:

Place fake booby traps around the flag. Anyone who touches them is considered hit and must return to the respawn.

# 17. My flag – your flag

## Complexity:

2 of 10

## Game environment:

long playground (gravel pit, meadow, wood, ...)

## Required:

- ✓ from 4 players
- ✓ 1-2 flags
- ✓ 1-2 pipes

## Game content:

- ➢ Position a flag in front of each respawn at 10 m distance.
- ➢ Split the players into two teams.
- ➢ Each team shall endeavor to conquer the opponent's flag and bring it into its own respawn.
- ➢ Players are free to carry and/or throw the flag.

   ### Attention:

   If the flag bearer is hit, he shall leave the flag on the spot and go to respawn. It is prohibited to move and/or throw the flag after a hit!

## Game objective:

Conquering the enemy flag! It counts who holds the flag in his hands at the end of the given time..

## Note for the administrator:

After the recapture, the own flag has to take the original place. It does not belong in your own respawn. Moving one's own flag is allowed after the opponent has conquered it!

Put the players under time pressure by limiting the game round to 10 - 30 minutes - considering the size of the location.

# 18. Pitch the »bomb«

## Complexity:

3 of 10

## Game environment:

open areas like meadown with coverings or gravel pit

## Required:

- ✓ from 4 players
  only "armed" with the sidearm
- ✓ 1 "bomb dummy"

## Game content:

- ➢ Place the dummy in the middle of the field.
- ➢ Split the players into two teams.
- ➢ Each team should make every effort to conquer the dummy and bring it into the foreign respawn.
- ➢ The players are free to carry and/or throw the dummy.

### Attention:

If the flag bearer is hit, he has to leave the dummy on the spot and go to the respawn. It is forbidden to move and/or throw the dummy after a hit!

## Game objective:

The team that brings the bomb dummy into the opposing respawn wins.

## *Note for the administrator:*

Good throwers can excel. A targeted throw into the respawn is valid! Make sure to make the dummy heavy, but not too heavy.

# 19. surrounded

## Complexity:

1 of 10

## Game environment:

wood, meadow, gravel pit, houses

## Required:

✓ from 4 players

## Game content:

➢ Split the players into two teams.

➢ Offers a team three options for a base to defend.

➢ Send them to the selected location.

➢ Send out the attackers 5 minutes later. Their task is to conquer Base.

➢ Every hit is a hit. There is one life per player.

## Game objective:

Conquest of the base.

## Note for the administrator:

This classic "Conquest Variant" is suitable for beginners as well as for amusing game fun in between.

If there are at least 3 machine guns among the players, divide these players to defend Base. Make sure that snipers come to the attackers.

Allow the defenders to expand Base better. For example, make filled sandbags available to them! The better the base is set up, the more the player ratio changes.

Give the attackers several lives if the defenders could massively strengthen their base.

# 20. the camp

## Complexity:

3 of 10

## Game environment:

wood, meadow, houses, gravel pit, ...

## Required:

- ✓ from 10 players up
- ✓ per »Camp« 1 marking (flag, Stick with coloured ribbon, ...)

## Game content:

- ➢ Distribute on both sides the same number of
- ➢ "Camps." Make sure that the "Camps" are as far away from the Respawns as possible!
- ➢ Split the players into two teams, inform them about their own camps«!
- ➢ The players' task is to take the camps and keep them. The number of players in the camp is limited to one person!!
- ➢ There is no respawn time for players!

## Game objective:

Whoever has taken all opposing camps first wins..

## Note for the administrator:

If you place the "Camps" too close to the Respawn, it makes sense to give the players a Respawntime. Limit the game time to 10 - 30 minutes - depending on the size of the game area.

*Variant:*

Allow the players to deactivate the camps. Give them "booby trap dummies", which they can use in the "Place "Camps.

# 21. King of the Hill!

## Complexity:

5 of 10

## Game environment:

meadow, gravel pit or generally terrain with a hill, hill or the like

## Required:

✓ from 4 players

## Game content:

➢ Divide the players into 2 teams.

➢ The player who reaches the hill first occupies it and then defends it against the other team.

➢ Each player gets 2 lives!

## Game objective:

Whoever has the hill in his possession after 30 minutes wins.

## Note for the administrator:

A Gravel pit! is ideally suited for this game mode. The terrain often changes as a result of the dismantling work and thus offers a variety of playing possibilities.

### Variant:

Divide the players into 4 or more teams. Give them

different respawn and let them choose them by a lot. Make sure that the respawns have different distances to the hill. Each team determines a "point man" with a life. As long as he is in the game, each member (except the "Pointman") has an unlimited number of lives. If the "Pointman" is hit, every player of this team has his last life!

# 22. Bomb the base

## Complexity:

4 of 10

## Game environment:

meadow, gravel pit

## Required:

- ✓ from 6 players
- ✓ alarm clock

## Game content:

➤ Divide the players into 2 teams.

*Attacker*:
Give this team the alarm clock and the task to blow up one of several possible points with the help of the alarm clock.

*Defender*:
They should thwart the attacker's plan.

➤ Before you send the teams to their respawn, give them the information about what points they are. Give them a few minutes to plan!

➤ Send the defense team into the playground to position themselves.

➢ After another 3 minutes, the attacking team will be cleared for take-off!

➢ If the attacking team makes it to one of the points, it places the alarm clock. The countdown is 5 Minutes! During this time the defenders may defuse the "alarm bomb"!

➢ If the alarm clock rings, the "alarm bomb" exploded!

## *Game objective:*

The attacking team wins if it blows up one of three possible points!

## *Note for the administrator:*

Each player gets a life! If the alarm bearer is hit, he has to set the alarm on the ground and go to the respawn. Defenders may pick up the alarm clock and bring it into their respawn. In this case, the defender wins automatically!

### *Variant:*

Distribute additional alarm clocks on the terrain. Set them to different times.

Each alarm clock that rings represent a bomb that has gone off and sends all players within a 3 m radius to the respawn. One of the "hit" players takes the "bomb" with him. If nobody is at the "alarm bomb" at this moment, the surrounding area (5 m radius) remains contaminated. Whoever stays in it, no matter how short, also loses his life. If you play in rooms, the "alarm bomb" applies to the entire room - no matter how big it is!

# 23. Oh Bomb!

## Complexity:

5 of 10

## Game environment:

Houses, Terrain with sufficient coverage possibilities

## Required:

- ✓ from 6 players
- ✓ 1 bomb dummy
- ✓ 1 circuit diagram

## Game content:

- ➢ Place the "alarm bomb" at any place on the game site. Make sure players hear the alarm clock unless they can find it in advance. Make sure that no player knows where the dummy is!

- ➢ Hide the circuit diagram separately on the site.

- ➢ Divide the players into 2 teams.

    *Team 1:*
    Has to defuse the bomb dummy.

    *Team 2:*
    Detonates the bomb dummy

- ➢ First, you have to find the bomb dummy. It can't be moved from its place!

- ➤ Either you try it out on good luck - that carries the risk of making the wrong decision! Or they are looking for the schematic of which they are informed at this moment!

- ➤ The team is allowed to split up so that one part remains with the bomb dummy for defense!

## Game objective:

The team whose task is completed wins - no matter by whom!

## Note for the administrator:

For this mode you need a bomb dummy that has 4 different states:

- o Normal
- o Neutral
- o Disarmed
- o "detonated"

If the players decide on "good luck" to defuse the bomb and it detonates, the opposing team wins automatically - and vice versa!

# 24. S.W.A.T.

## Complexity:

4 of 10

## Game environment:

large house with 2 - 4 entrances - independent access

## Required:

- ✓ from 6 players
- ✓ Barricade material
- ✓ 1 "safe" to hide the case
- ✓ "Mines"
- ✓ Case (optimal with a combination lock and the possibility to fix it on the wrist)
- ✓ envelope
- ✓ Signs with the wording "SWAT"

## Game content:

- ➤ Split the players into two teams.

    *SWAT-Kommando*:

    should arrest the criminals

    *Specialists for art theft*
    want to steal something valuable

Defending the suitcase until it is open

➤ Send the specialists to the house. They are allowed to use it with all available materials ("mines and barricade up to the junk. At the same time, they should find the safe with the suitcase.

➤ Send the SWAT command into the building after 5 minutes.

➤ One of the specialists tries to open the suitcase. His team members shield him from attack by the SWAT command. Once the suitcase is open, they have to flee.

➤ At the same time, the SWAT command tries to obtain the suitcase or at least the contents of the suitcase.

➤ If a specialist is hit, he remains out of action until another specialist "heals" him. If a SWAT command heals a specialist, the specialist is regarded as

➤ "arrested" and goes to prison (the respawn of SWAT Command).

## Game objective:

It wins the side that brings the envelope into its own respawn!  The SWAT command also succeeds if the specialists do not steal the envelope.

## Note for the administrator:

If the "healer" (second cycle) has counted up to 20, the other player is healed!

---

# 25. Samurai vs. Ninja

## Complexity:

9 of 10

## Game environment:

open spaces, Houses, Halls

particular feature

Twilight or night

## Required:

- ✓ darkened play location or 2 night hours
- ✓ Teams at a ratio of 2 to 1
- ✓ 3 players or more divided between teams
- ✓ Rubber knives, latex swords, ...
- ✓ 1 map of the playing area
- ✓ Flags or high poles

## Game content:

- ➢ Form two teams in the ratio 2 to 1 - on 2 Ninja comes to 1 Samurai!

    ### Attacker/Samurai:

    armed with Airsoft markers

    Conquering predefined points/positions

_Verteidiger/Ninja_:

 armed with rubber knives, latex swords, ...

 -> NO markers

 Defense of pre-defined points/positions

## Game objective:

Conquering pre-defined points/positions or eliminating the opposing side

## Note for the administrator:

The difficulty of this game mode lies in the limited view! At the same time, this is exactly the reason for the attraction! Wait until dusk or nightfall. Alternatively, it is sufficient to darken a Hall! Important for the game mode "Samurai vs. Ninja" is a darkened game location!

### Determination of points:

Select a few points of the game location that the samurai have to conquer. Mark these points on a map and tell the players about these positions. The marking of the positions by immovable flags or high sticks is well suited.

### Attention:

Discuss the hit regulation with the players in advance! Keep in mind that Ninja does not carry markers with them - but act in "close combat"!

# 26. Zombies!!!

## Complexity:

9 of 10

## Game environment:

open areas, houses, halls

*particular failure*

Twilight or night

## Required:

- ✓ From 4 players up
- ✓ per Hunter one note with one task

## Game content:

- ➢ Form two teams!

  *Hunter*

  Receive of the game management orders handed out, which are to be fulfilled

  *Zombies*

  pass Hunter off and transform her into your equals

- ➢ Send the zombies to the playground to find a hiding place.

- ➢ Give the hunters the task sheets. Let them read them and explain if necessary!

- ➢ After 5 - 10 minutes, send the hunters to the field to complete their tasks.

➢ On the way to their tasks, the Zombies wait! If a zombie touches them, the Hunters have to put their markers away - they are also zombies from this moment on!

➢ If a zombie is hit, it won't move for 30 seconds. In this state, it may not attack or be attacked.

## Game objective:

Fulfillment of the tasks by the Hunter or the transformation of the Hunter into Zombies!

## Note for the administrator:

Give the hunters different missions right at the beginning of the mission. These have to be done!

On the way to the task, they have to move through dark areas - anytime exposed to the risk of being attacked by zombies. If a zombie is hit, it may move the next 30 seconds only on all fours crawling forward or no longer move. In this state, he may no longer be attacked. Hunter, of Zombies, touched, instantly turn into a zombie and change sides!

The difficulty of this game mode lies in the limited view! At the same time, exactly this circumstance holds the attraction!

Wait until dusk or nightfall!

### Definition of orders:

Prepare orders of your choice, vary them from game to game, that gives the whole thing more fun!

*Attention:*

Discuss the hit rules with the players in advance!
Remember that zombies don't use markers - they act in
close combat!

# 27. Simon says ...

## Complexity:

5 of 10

## Game environment:

meadow, wood, gravel pit, houses, halls, ...

## Required:

✓ from 4 players

✓ the tasks set determine the required material

## Game content:

➤ Choose a player as "leader" to give the commands.

➤ The players have to position themselves behind the "leader". The "leader" gives the commands at will.

### Tasks/Command:

-> Reload within a short time

-> Change stop positions

-> fire (single shot or continuous fire)

-> Coverage types

-> imitate hand signals

-> forward - jump - cover

he commands are to be executed when the

"leader" puts the words "Simon says..." ahead.

Who executes a command without the words

"Simon says..." is out of the question.

Anyone who executes a wrong command is eliminated.

➢ Anyone who does not execute a command is eliminated.

➢ If there is a technical problem or if the player cannot execute the command for other reasons, the movement sequence must be simulated in the best possible way. In this case the player remains in the race.

## Game objective:

The last player in the game wins. The

"Leader" is thus a person outside of the

"Survival radius".

## Note for the administrator:

Be sure to explain the commands to the appointed "leader" before the game. Give him the opportunity to use other commands as he pleases.

### Referral:

This game mode is great for tuning up a team in general and for practicing commands!

### Variant:

The "leader" faces the players and looks at them. He doesn't do the movements, he just gives the commands.

# 28. fight like a general!

## Complexity:

4 of 10

## Game environment:

wood, meadow, gravel pit, ...

## Required:

✓ From 10 players

## Game content:

➤ Divide the players into two teams.

➤ Let the players compete in two lines on each side.

➤ The fight follows in the style of classic armies:

-> row 1 kneels, row 2 loads a single BB

-> row 1 shoots!

-> Row 2 moves forward!

-> row 2 kneels, row 1 loads single BB

➤ Players hit to leave the playground.

## Game objective:

The side that has players wins!

## Note for the administrator:

This game is about the accuracy, not speed! Be sure to choose a clear terrain, you'll be in command of the shots.

Shoot players before your command, these are to disqualify!

In this game mode, there are no MGs and no pure continuous fire markers. This mode can be sharpened if you only allow sidearms.

# 29. »Football«

## Complexity:

6 of 10

## Game environment:

Wood, Meadow, Houses, Halls, rather open surfaces - suitable for "Speed games«

## Required:

- ✓ from 8 - 10 players
- ✓ something that marks the gates (sticks with loud ribbons, flags, ...)
- ✓ 1 American football or classic football

## Game content:

- ➤ Divide the playing field into 4 zones of approximately equal size.
- ➤ Place the goals in front of the respawn, make sure you have a suitable size (5-20 m depending on the playground)!
- ➤ Place the ball in the middle of the field.
- ➤ Ball rules:

    *Pick up the ball:*

    Throws apply backward or sideways.

    *Kicking balls:*

permitted in any direction

➢ Players who carry the ball and receive hits drop the ball immediately. Your respawn lasts 20 seconds.

➢ All players without a ball are allowed to return to the game immediately!

## Game objective:

As in "American Football", the ball must pass over the opponent's goal line!

## Note for the administrator:

Each player has 2 lives!

This game mode easily leans on the rules of the

"American football." If you know the rules and can teach them to the players, you may tighten this game mode accordingly!

This game mode is ideal for humorous interludes in the form of "Cheerleaders". Organize typical cheerleader pompoms and let each player in respawn swing the pompoms for a new life and call a spontaneous and/or creative cheer like a cheerleader.

Acrobatic exercises make little or no sense due to the typical airsoft equipment.

These "cheerleaders" dare with the pompons on the playing field and behave like "cheerleaders" they may bring three players of their team extra life. It is forbidden to shoot at the "cheerleaders"!

# 30. survive the game

## Complexity:

8 of 10

## Game environment:

meadow, wood, houses

## Required:

- ✓ 6 – 15 players
- ✓ different loop colors

## Game content:

- ➢ 1 single player volunteers!

    *Runners:*
    1-3 players remain in players

    *police:*
    2 / 3 of the remaining players

    *hunter:*
    1 / 3 of the remaining players

- ➢ The runners hide on the site. Their task is to eliminate their pursuers. They may defend themselves, but not attack!

- ➢ First, the hunters start to search and hunt the runners.

- ➢ 15 minutes later the police players enter the field. From this moment on, the hunters are the fugitives.

➤ If the runners meet policemen, they are out. The policemen "save" the runners and hunt the hunters at the same time.

## Game objective:

The runners have 1 hour to survive.

## Note for the administrator:

Every hit player leaves the game area after a hit. There is no respawn, everyone has a life.

### Referral:

Inform the players sufficiently about the respective tasks:

- ✓ *runners:*
  Hide, hunter, help the policemen and save them

- ✓ *hunter:*
  Hunted of the policemen and in search of runner

- ✓ *police:*
  Rescue runners and eliminate hunters

### Variant:

Vary the game time and leave the players in the game until all hunters are out of the game.

# 31. Headhunter

## Complexity:

3 of 10

## Game environment:

Wood, Meadow, Halls, Houses

## Required:

- ✓ from 7 players
- ✓ 60 smaller notes, on each note a number from 1 - 20
- ✓ Container for drawing warps

## Game content:

- ➤ Select 1 Assistant and post it to the Respawn. The wizard's task is to note the points correctly.

- ➤ Select several players and let them draw the notes until nobody can find them in the container anymore. Equipped with this, these targets hide on the terrain.

- ➤ 5 minutes later the other players follow.

- ➤ If a player detects and hits a target, this is considered a hit. He or she receives a piece of paper from the target person and brings this piece of paper to the assistant of the administrator.

- ➤ Players are allowed to hunt down other players with the notes and take them away.

> If a target has no more paper, he leaves the playing field!

## Game objective:

The player with the highest score wins.

## Note for the administrator:

There is no respawn time. Any player who enters the respawn will leave it immediately.

### Variant:

Allow the targets to defend themselves. If a target hits a player, he has to wait for 30 seconds at the assistant.

Let the target start wave by wave. For this Variant, you need a powerful toad. With each blast, a target enters the game.

Give each target a camouflage net, which they put down as soon as they hear "their" toad symbol sound. You collect the camo net after the game. Instead of the toad, there is a timer for each target. Set them to different times.

When the timer time expires, the game begins for them.

# 32. tanks

## Complexity:

3 of 10

## Game environment:

meadow, gravel pit, area with houses

## Required:

- ✓ from 6 players
- ✓ 1 tank model made of cardboard or papier mache, with several targets
- ✓ 1 map with 6 points

## Game content:

- ➢ Divide the players into 2 teams.

  ### Team tanks:

  They man the tank. They are primarily protected by the tank.

  ### Attacker:

  Elimination of the tank

- ➢ The tank team receives the map with the marked points. Point A is their starting point and respawn. Your route is determined by the points on the map!

- ➢ The attacking team is given the task of eliminating all targets on the tank and thus "unfit to drive".

## Game objective:

The game mode ends when the tank has reached the target or the attackers have eliminated the tank.

## Note for the administrator:

A shell that resembles a rudimentary tank optically is sufficient as a dummy tank. Aluminum foils attached to it represent the targets. The game mode ends positively for the attackers with a hit on the last target.

Fix a sequence of points on the map. On average 6 pieces are well suited. The bigger the terrain, the more points the map may have. The tank has to score all points:

Starting point A - continue to B - continue to C, D, E,... Put the points in the zigzag pattern. The last point is near the respawn of the attacking team.

### Variant:

At each station, there is a task to complete before the tank is allowed to continue. In this case, the respawn of the tank team changes. If the tank reaches point B and the task is completed positively, the new respawn point B is reached. The tank team is allowed to reject a task, in which case the respawn remains at the previous position.

# 33. Drawn!

## Complexity:

5 of 10

## Game environment:

meadow, gravel pit, halls, houses

## Required:

- ✓ from 6 players
- ✓ per player 1 pin and 1 small note container for the notes
- ✓ 1 assistant or helper in the safe zone

## Game content:

- ➤ Let each player draw a piece of paper. On the piece of paper is the team of the player in this round! They have to keep their team to themselves for the time being!

- ➤ Your helper notes who belongs to which team!

- ➤ Afterward, collect the notes again and announce the slogans to them:

  Team A–> attack

  Team B–> protect

- ➤ The players distribute themselves as they please across the playing area. There is no concrete starting point!

  *Task 1:*

Find out which player belongs to your team!

*Challenge 2:*

Elimination of the opposing team!

➢ It is up to the players how they get to the slogans of the others. Players of the same team join together. Players of the opposing team open fire on each other. The first player to be hit leaves the field. In this case, it is important to adhere to the hit rule!

➢ Players in demand who belong to the opposing team do not have to answer, but may immediately answer the questioner "HITen"!

## Game objective:

Only Member of Team A or Team B can be found on the site.

## Note for the administrator:

Label half of the pieces of paper with Team A and Team B or with 2 different team names (Eagle and Falcon, Fox and hen, Korea and Vietnam, USA and USSR,...).

Fold them together and put them in the container.

The same applies to the slogans Attack and Protection. Choose other terms on request. Important is memorability and a short number of syllables!

*How do the players find out who belongs together?*

o Questions and hope for the best

o From ambush to another hold the marker in the

back and ask

- ○ Wait until other players are nearby and listen to them

- ○ Creative, own solutions

- ○ Your helper in the safe zone waits for the players who have been shot out. If all players of a team from the game are in the safe zone, he gives the signal for the end of the game.

*Variant:*

There is no respawn, the players have an infinite number of lives. Each time they hit, they go back to the safe zone and draw a new ticket. Your helper notes the current status!

The winner after a certain time is the team with the most players on the field! In this case a fixed 50:50 division of the players are NOT given any longer!

If you have enough players available, the option is Team 3.

This team receives an Airsoft hand grenade. Whoever is hit by an Airsoft hand grenade has forfeited his last life and is not allowed to draw another lot.

# Scenarios

Were you already a member of a MilSim?

MilSim's favorite topics are rescue missions, bomb disposal or the elimination of enemy rulers. The duration varies from a few hours to several days.

MilSims are based on real events and actual military missions. This doesn't mean putting the players in danger - but giving them a feeling for real missions! Players such as "real military" without being exposed to the dangers of it.

MilSims usually contain concrete scenarios. In contrast to pure "speed game" game modes, they are more complex and contain antagonists of real or fictitious nations!

### *Scenarios are interchangeable!*

- o You will not only find nuclear power plants in Chernobyl!
- o Kidnapping scenarios are just as suitable for Afghanistan as they are for Philippine waters.
- o Hidden pirate treasures can be found in the Caribbean - or in the far north like the Nibelungen treasure!

If you don't like a scenario, change it. Choose an alternative world, a fictional country or an alternative "Terror target"! Just make sure that it harmonizes in itself!

- o You are the master of your world!
- o You are the creator!

- You tell the story!

As good authors know, it doesn't only depend on the story, but also on the background. A well-chosen scenario is as essential as Required equipment.

With it, you create a background in front of which the players act, into which they put themselves and which gives them a red thread.

Be aware of this, you give them the tools, they are the heroes of their own story.

_Which scenarios are interesting for your players?_

_Have you ever asked them?_

You'll be amazed to see how different the ideas and creativity are in Airsoft players.

# 34. Radioaktive

## Complexity:

5 of 10

## Game environment:

meadow, wood, gravel pit, houses, halls, ...

## Required:

- ✓ from 6 players
- ✓ Suitcase with documents
- ✓ per player 1 - 2 smaller boxes filled with sand Gauze bandages as required

## Scenario:

### Russia - in a few years:

The government plans to shut down a power plant. Daof heard of a handful of terrorists planning to steal weapons-grade plutonium from the power plant. They wait for the preparatory phase and attack during the loading phase

## Game content:

➢ Split the players into 3 teams..

### Team 1: Guarding the nuclear power plant

They monitor the building complex, the plutonium and protect important documents on the Russian nuclear program.

If the theft of plutonium is successful, they will participate. the guards will join the search operation and support the soldiers.

### *Team 2: Terrorists*

Well-trained mercenaries who would sell their own grandmother for money. Their job is to steal plutonium and documents. If both are in their possession, they fight their way back to the pick-up zone.

### *Team 3: Soldiers*

They are to collect plutonium and documents. If the soldiers have plutonium and documents, the guards accompany the soldiers to the starting point.

➢ Plutonium and documents are in the middle of the playing field.

➢ Send the guards away!

➢ 1 minute later terrorists and soldiers start from the opposite side of the field.

➢ Plutonium and document cases must be worn - throwing is forbidden! If the carrier is hit, he drops both.

## *Game objective:*

Soldiers and guards win when they have brought both to safety.

Terrorists win when plutonium and documents are in their respawn.

## _Note for the administrator:_

You can fill the boxes with anything you can, provided they get weight.

- o Soldiers don't have paramedics, but they can access the guards' paramedics.

- o Guards can have a paramedic, the group decides for itself. If they decide for a medic, then this may supply the soldiers if necessary.

- o Terrorists have excellent training, so everyone has two gauze bandages. This allows him to "treat" himself or another player. The "Healing phase" lasts until the gauze bandage is completely wrapped.

### _Variant:_
Put the documents in the suitcase and pack the plutonium in a heavy chest, which can only be carried by two people.

# 35. Scavenger hunt on the Pirate treasure!

## Complexity:

8 of 10

## Game environment:

Wood – the terrain has to be large enough

## Required:

- ✓ from 4 players
- ✓ 1 treasure chest in old pirate style
- ✓ 1 treasure map
- ✓ several hints for finding the treasure map
- ✓ 2x block and writing utensils

## Scenario:

### Caribbean:

Treasure hunters received information about an unsecured pirate treasure. Interested they go on a search without realizing at first that they are not the only ones! Time hurts!

## Game content:

➢ Hide the treasure chest on the playground and camouflage it with a thin layer of earth.

- Find a suitable place to hide the treasure map. Build clues in the style of a scavenger hunt.

- Divide the players into 2 teams.

- Share the first puzzle with the players. Give each player a writing pad and writing materials.

- The players need time to solve the puzzles. Send them to the respawn and wait 5 minutes until they are ready to start.

- Players must bring the treasure chest they have found into their own respawn.

- If you carry the chest, you are not allowed to use markers! If a hit is made, the wearer must place the chest on the ground and visit the respawn.

## Game objective:

The team that brings the treasure chest into its own respawn wins.

## Note for the administrator:

Adjust the level of difficulty and the number of puzzles to the players. The puzzles lead the players to the place with the following puzzle.

### Variant:

Players may not play opposing players and ask for information about the opponent's position.

---

# 36. Save the President!

## Complexity:

3 of 10

## Game environment:

wood, meadow, gravel pit, houses, halls

## Required:

✓ from 8 players

## Scenario:

### Afghanistan a few years ago:

A group under the leadership of a warlord experienced the diplomatic journey of a president. The warlord recognizes his capture as high leverage. They shoot the plane down, whereupon it makes an emergency landing. The president and his bodyguards survive but are forced to get to safety.

## Game content:

➤ Let a lottery ticket decide who will play the role of the "President" takes over. This player stands by your side. He is forbidden to use markers!

➤ Divide the remaining players into 2 groups.

### Bodyguards:

They protect the president and have to move him to a

pre-determined place.

### Attacker:

They try to eliminate the President before he reaches the safe place.

➢ Send the attackers into their respawn.

➢ The president and his bodyguards start from a point on the field to simulate the emergency landing. They must make their way to a previously announced point!

## Game objective:

The President arrives alive at the predetermined point!

## Note for the administrator:

Players with Russian Airsoft models automatically join the group of attackers. Each attacker gets 5 lives, the bodyguards and their president one. If you have enough players, there are 4 bodyguards for every 1 attacker. Otherwise, divide at your discretion!

### Variant:

Instead of Afghanistan, you can send a troop of attackers to the "Parliament". In this case, the division turns around.

The majority of the players provide security personnel. In this variant, all players have the same number of lives.

The president receives a weapon of his choice, which can be used for

"Emergencies" is deposited in Parliament!

# 37. pilot rescue

## Complexity:

2 of 10

## Game environment:

wood, meadow, gravel pit, houses, halls

## Required:

✓ from 8 players

## Scenario:

### Nigeria - a few years ago:

In the war zone, a group of fighters meets the plane of an aid organization. The pilot rescues himself from the crashed plane. How does he get back to the safe area?

His colleagues did not survive the crash. The pilot has no weapons except a sidearm and an extra magazine, which he takes from his colleague.

The missionaries he was supposed to take the cargo to await his arrival and send a rescue team on their way after they learn of the crash! Until this team arrives, the pilot must primarily hide!

## Game content:

➢ Let a lot decide who takes on the role of "pilot".

➢ Send the pilot to the terrain and give him 10 minutes to

hide!

➤ Divide the players into 2 teams.

*Rescue team:*

Find the pilot and bring him to the respawn.

*Team 2:*

Locals who plan to capture the pilot.

## Game objective:

Rescue of the pilot.

## Note for the administrator:

Each player gets 3 lives. If the pilot is hit, the game is over immediately!

*Variant:*

In this variant the pilot gets a rubber or latex knife. Give each player a piece of paper. These notes symbolize extra ammunition.

For each piece of paper the pilot gets, he has an extra magazine at his disposal. He receives the notes if he manages to knife a player of the "local team". In this case, the player hands over the piece of paper and gets a new one for his next life in respawning.

# 38. Little Princess

## Complexity:

10 of 10

## Game environment:

wood, meadow, gravel pit, houses, halls

## Required:

- ✓ From 4 players
- ✓ 1 woman or someone who disguises himself as a woman three bags of flour (simulates the drugs)
- ✓ 1 note with a message from the drug baron

## Scenario:

### Mexico - Fight against the drug cartel:

In the middle of Mexico, the kidnapping of a student makes headlines. The daughter of a high-ranking

"Drug barons" disappeared overnight and haven't turned up since. A troop of fighters is charged with their rescue after the father receives the first ransom extortions to his father, he sends his best fighters!

## Game content:

Bring the puppet or the player/actress into the

"Prison Camp" (the kidnappers' respawn). Stell

"Little Princess a plastic knife and give her three bags of flour. She has to hide these "drugs" in the surrounding area!

➢ Divide the players into 2 teams.

*Rescue team:*

Plan the liberation of the "Little Princess".

*Kidnappers:*

Blackmail the drug baron and hold his daughter captive.

are to find out where "Little Princess" is holding the

"Drug bag" was hiding

"Little Princess" dares to make his own escape attempts in the course of the game. The hijacking team finds ropes on them respawn that they can easily knock down, allowing them to simulate "bondage".

If she is alone in the respawn, "Little Princess" counts up to 30 each time, removes her shackles and tries to flee all the time.

If she manages to escape, her guards are allowed to catch her. A light touch on the shoulder and the comment "come along" is enough.

## *Game objective:*

Rescue of the "Little Princess".

## Note for the administrator:

"Little Princess" tries to escape. With her plastic knife, she can attack her kidnappers inside the Respawn. If she touches a player on the torso near her heart with the knife, that player is out of the game!

If the "kidnappers" think about guarding her and turn their backs on her, she may count to 60 and try again to kick her "guards" out of the game.

The "kidnappers" are allowed to ask her for drugs. Little Princess" has to reveal the hiding places truthfully! If "Little Princess" is on her escape into the fire and gets a hit, she is out of the game and the game would be over. If the "kidnappers" know about the "drug bags", they get another chance! The guards are also allowed to ask "Little Princess" about hidden "weapons". She has to answer truthfully and hand over the "weapons". However, she may get her "weapons" back if she frees herself and does not watch her guards.

If the rescue team finds all three bags, they may hand them over to the kidnappers in exchange for "Little Princess". This is considered a rescue, provided that the

"Kidnappers" go for it!

### Important:

> If "Little Princess" is hit at a BB, the game is automatically over! In this case, there are no winners or losers - but a draw.

# 39. the village

## Complexity:

7 of 10

## Game environment:

several Houses with Wood

## Required:

- ✓ 6 – 30 players
- ✓ 1 ribbon for the guerrilla leader

## Scenario:

### In the heart of Africa - in the last decades:

In the middle of a tiny village exists the only source of water within a radius of dozens of kilometers. A few fighters protect the village from a group of "guerrillas" who want to recapture "their" village.

## Game content:

➢ Divide the players into 2 teams.

➢ Send team 1 (defender) into the game area.

➢ For them, the paramedic rule applies! If their points are used up, they have to leave the game area.

➢ Team 2 selects 1 - 3 players from its ranks (depending on player strength) into the "supply troop". The "Supply Squad" stays out of the game for now. Furthermore, they draw a player, who is the

➤ "Guerrilla Leader" acts!

## Game objective:

The reconquest of the village or elimination of the

"Guerrilla Leader".

## Note for the administrator:

There is no respawn for the team in the village. Instead, they get a hit list! With 10 hitpoints they are out of the game!

*Hits in arms and legs:* 1 point

*Hit into the torso (front and back):* 4 points

*Headhits:* 2 points and they stay on the ground for 10 seconds!

Attackers have unlimited lives. They may only return to the game after at least 1 other player has respawned!

Give the "Supply Troop" a container with smaller items that serve as "supply".

This squad brings ammo, food and medical supplies to the attackers! The players of the "Supply Troop" have one life.

The "Guerilla Leader" has 1 life! If he gets a hit, he may name a successor. The player joins the troop again as a "normal" guerilla. If the successor also gets a hit, he names another player as his successor. As soon as the 3rd "Guerilla Leader" gets a hit, the game is over!

# 40. Résistance

## Complexity:

5 of 10

## Game environment:

meadow, gravel pit, wood

## Required:

- ✓ from 10 players
- ✓ 1 Map with coordinates
- ✓ 2 Cubes
- ✓ Loops for three teams

## Scenario:

### France – 1944:

On the way to the Resistance, a handful of SOE agents land in the middle of nowhere. Their task is to salvage notes from German scientists who are currently hidden on the site.

## Game content:

- ➢ Hide an object (chest, suitcase, ...) somewhere on the playing field. You will find the documents you are looking for!
- ➢ Divide the players into 3 teams.
- ➢ Let each "SOE agent" throw his landing coordinates away from the others.

- ➢ Send the "SOE agents" to the field. They take their places based on the landing coordinates.

- ➢ Résistance and French army start at the same time from their respective respawn.

- ➢ The searches the game area for the

- ➢ "SOE agents" and together they search for the hidden object. The French army wants to prevent both.

- ➢ If the object is found, it must get into the Respawn of the Résistance.

  *Attention:*

  If the carrier is hit, he has to leave the object on the spot and go to the Respawn. It is forbidden to move and/or throw after a hit!

## Game objective:

The documents get into the Respawn of the Résistance.

## Note for the administrator:

You need 3 teams in this game mode:

- o SOE Agents (30%) - use the Respawn of the Résistance

- o Résistance (20%)

- o french army (50%)!

Give to the players of the French army before starting the game half of the landing coordinates are known.

# Rules of the game

It is up to the game management to what extent these basic rules are used. Feel free to change and modify them according to your own ideas or to omit them completely.

Explain the rules to the participants in your games before each game day. You will avoid discrepancies and misunderstandings!

## paramedic rule

Each side has at least one player who acts as a paramedic. Players who have been hit lie down on the ground and wait until the paramedic arrives. It is allowed to call for the paramedic!

A short touch of the paramedic is enough to get the player back into action. If the paramedic is unable to reach the injured player within 3 minutes, the player leaves the field.

## Respawn rul

If players have more than one life, they "regenerate" in respawn. With their hand raised and their marker secured, they hurry back into their own respawn. They wear a light cloth or warning vest to signal their return to respawn.

When they arrive there, they touch a wooden peg, wall or other point and immediately rush back into the game.

## Marker rule

If a BB hits the marker, the player remains "alive". He doesn't need to respawn! This does not apply to the marker. In this round he has no further option to bet - he is "lost".

If the player has it, he continues to play with his sidearm or "knives" if he has a plastic and/or latex knife. SHOTs with the marker hit do not apply!

## Minimum distance rule

Shooting below a minimum distance is prohibited.

Open terrain:

✓ Normal markers - 10 m

✓ Sniper rifles - 25 m

In closed rooms the minimum distance is shorter!

Below these distances the player points with the marker at the opponent and screams "SHOT" to signal the shot!

If he does not point with the marker at the opponent, the following applies "SHOT" not!

## Knife rule

Individual players carry a plastic or latex knife to improve the appearance of their display.

If a player manages to sneak up on his opponent, he is allowed to "knife". A light touch with the knife is enough - the opponent is put out of action!

# Epilogue

Don't be afraid to develop your own ideas!
Try out what you can think of, test something new, orientate yourself on computer games or films - it's up to you. No matter what you plan, think about rudimentary basics. If it's a new mode, let the players test it! Then ask them what they think. You profit from it! What should be taken into account when developing a new product?

- ✓ Which playground is available?

- ✓ How many players can I expect?

- ✓ Are there players or volunteers who want to represent independent characters (shot down pilots, the president, ...)?

- ✓ What is your game mode about?

- ✓ What equipment do you need?

- ✓ Do you set a certain timeframe?

- ✓ Do you plan different variations?

- ✓ How complex do you plan the game mode?

- ✓ How do you plan to "entertain" the players?

Try it out, most players will quickly get enthusiastic about innovative ideas. Be the game leader players want - let them be the hero in their own story!

# Game modes

1. Last man standing ..................................9

2. One in the Chamber...............................10

3. Lonely Wolf...........................................12

4. find the Terrorist ..................................14

5. Counterkill-Parcour ..............................16

6. Vietnam...............................................18

7. gladiator fight .....................................20

8. Team Deathmatch – TMD........................22

9. Respawn Deathmatch ...........................23

10. Sniper and Spotter...............................25

11. Collect it! ...........................................26

12. Wolfpack .............................................28

13. Tree changes!......................................30

14. Captainshunt ......................................30

15. Capture the flag...................................32

16. battle for the flag ................................34

17. My flag – your flag ...............................36

18. Pitch the »bomb«.................................38

19. surrounded .........................................40

20.  the camp ...........................................42

21. *King of the Hill!* ....................................................44

22. *Bomb the base* .....................................................46

23. *Oh Bomb!* ...........................................................48

24. *S.W.A.T.* ............................................................50

25. *Samurai vs. Ninja* ...............................................52

26. *Zombies!!!* ..........................................................54

27. *Simon says* ...........................................................57

28. *fight like a general!* ...........................................60

29. *»Football«* ..........................................................62

30. *survive the game* ................................................64

31. *Headhunter* ........................................................66

32. *tanks* ................................................................68

33. *Drawn!* ..............................................................70

34. *Radioaktive* ........................................................75

35. *Scavenger hunt on the Pirate treasure!* .................78

36. *Save the President!* .............................................80

37. *pilot rescue* ........................................................82

38. *Little Princess* .....................................................84

39. *the village* ..........................................................87

40. *Résistance* ..........................................................89